Kids in the Kitchen™
The Library of Multicultural Cooking

food and recipes of greece

by Theresa M. Beatty

The Rosen Publishing Group's
PowerKids Press™
New York

The recipes in this book are intended for a child to make together with an adult.
Many thanks to Ruth Rosen and her test kitchen.

Published in 1999 by The Rosen Publishing Group, Inc.
29 East 21st Street, New York, NY 10010

Copyright © 1999 by The Rosen Publishing Group, Inc.

First Edition

Book Design: Resa Listort

Photo Credits and Illustrations: p. 7 © J.G. Edmanson/International Stock; pp. 8,10 © John Novajosky; p. 9 © Christine Innamorato; pp. 11, 19, 21 © Pablo Maldonado; p. 12 © Mark Bolster/International Stock; p.13 © Peter Johansky/FPG International; p. 15 © Mike Malyszko/FPG International; p. 16 © Robert Cundy/FPG International; pp. 18, 20 © Ira Fox.

Beatty, Theresa M.
    Food and Recipes of Greece / by Theresa M. Beatty.
       p.   cm. — (Kids in the kitchen : multicultural cooking)
    Includes index.
    Summary: Describes some of the foods enjoyed in Greece and provides recipes for several popular Greek dishes.
    ISBN 0-8239-5223-1
    1. Cookery, Greek—Juvenile literature. 2. Food habits—Greece—Juvenile literature. [1. Food habits—Greece. 2. Cookery—Greek] I. Title. II.
Series: Beatty, Theresa M. Kids in the kitchen.
    TX723.5.G8B43 1998
    641.59495—dc21
                                      98-11741
                                            CIP
                                          AC

Manufactured in the United States of America

contents

Abbreviations

cup = c. Farenheit = F. tablespoon = tbsp. teaspoon = tsp.

Celsius = C. kilogram = kilo liter = l milliliter = ml

GREECE

MARMARA DENIZI

AEGEAN SEA

IONIAN SEA

SEA OF CRETE

MEDITERRANEAN SEA

GREECE

Greece is a rocky, seaside country in southern Europe. The mainland of Greece is surrounded by the Mediterranean Sea. Over 1,400 small islands are also part of Greece.

Northwestern Greece has many mountains and the weather can be very cool at times. Crete, the largest Greek island, lies so far to the south of the mainland that the weather there can be very hot. Most of Greece, however, enjoys warm summers and mild winters.

The Greek **civilization** (SIH-vih-lih-ZAY-shun) is thousands of years old. Yet modern Greeks eat some of the very same foods that ancient Greeks did long ago. These foods include grains, olives and olive oil, and fresh fruits and vegetables.

◀ *Greece is surrounded by the Aegean, Ionian, and Cretan Seas, all of which are part of the Mediterranean Sea.*

the cuisine of greece

Greek **cuisine** (kwih-ZEEN) is very healthful. Greeks and other peoples of the Mediterranean area eat red meat, such as beef or lamb, only a few times a month. Breads, pasta, rice, grains, and potatoes are eaten almost every day. Beans, fruits, nuts, and vegetables are also enjoyed daily as is olive oil. Cheese, such as feta, and yogurt are also eaten every day. Fish, chicken, and eggs are eaten a few times a week. All of these things keep the Greek diet low in animal fat, which comes from things like red meat, and high in **nutrients** (NOO-tree-ints) that keep people healthy.

In Greece, food is meant to be enjoyed and shared with others. It is also a big part of religious holidays, which are very important in Greece.

Dining outdoors is very common in Greece because many parts of Greece are warm and sunny most of the year. ▶

influences from many lands

Many **cultures** (KUL-cherz) have influenced Greek cooking. Throughout history, when people from other lands such as Italy, Turkey, Morocco, and the Middle East came to Greece, they brought some of their own foods and cooking styles with them. And when Greeks visited other places, they brought new and interesting foods back to Greece with them.

The Greeks also got some of their food from the Americas. When Europeans **explored** (eks-PLORD) North America and South America about 500 years ago, they brought back tomatoes and potatoes, which are now common ingredients in many Greek recipes.

Greek Salad

you will need:

For the Salad:

½ head Iceburg lettuce, torn by hand into small pieces

1 c. *(250 ml)* shredded red cabbage

1 clove garlic, finely chopped

1 cucumber, peeled and thinly sliced

8 cherry tomatoes

1 onion, thinly sliced

2 green or red bell peppers, thinly sliced into rings

15–20 Greek olives, pitted

¼ to ⅓ lb. *(.12 to .15 kilo)* crumbled feta cheese

For the Dressing:

½ cup *(125 ml)* olive oil

3 tbsp. *(40 ml)* red wine vinegar

1 tsp. *(5 ml)* lemon juice

½ tsp. *(2 ml)* oregano

½ tsp. *(2 ml)* salt

dash of black pepper

how to do it:

the salad:

■ Combine lettuce, cabbage, garlic, cucumber, tomatoes, peppers, onions, Greek olives, and feta cheese in a large salad bowl. Toss well.

■ Pour dressing over salad and toss well enough to coat ingredients.

the dressing:

■ Pour oil , lemon juice, and vinegar into a glass bottle

■ Add salt and pepper, cover bottle, and shake.

■ Add oregano and shake well.

■ Serve with warm pita bread.

Serves 4

Always ask a grown-up to help you when using knives!
Always ask a grown-up to help you when using the stove or oven!

9

the midday meal

In big Greek cities, like Athens, people aren't always able to go home to eat during the day as people can who live in small towns and villages. Whether they go home or to a **taverna** (tah-VER-nuh), many people enjoy their biggest and most important meal of the day in the middle of the afternoon. Shops close, people leave work, and children are let out of school so that people can gather for the midday meal.

Olives, yogurt, vegetables, fruits, bread, and pasta are some of the things that are served. This relaxed feast gives friends and families a chance to spend time together.

tzatziki
(cucumber-yogurt sauce)

you will need:

2 c. (500 ml) plain
   yogurt
1 unpeeled cucumber,
   finely chopped
2 cloves garlic,
   crushed
2 tbsp. (30 ml) olive oil
1 tsp. (5 ml) salt

how to do it:

- In a bowl, add the cucumber, garlic, olive oil, and salt to the yogurt. Blend well with a fork. Refrigerate.

- Serve with toasted pieces of pita bread or fresh vegetables, such as carrots, celery, or peppers.

Makes 2½ cups or 625 ml.

Always ask a grown-up to help you when using knives!
Always ask a grown-up to help you when using the stove or oven!

Greek foods

Fresh food is such a big part of Greek cuisine that almost every town has a couple of open markets. There the bins and stalls overflow with freshly caught seafood and colorful fruits and vegetables.

Cucumbers, lemons, peppers, spinach, and tomatoes are all **staples** (STAY-pulz) of Greek cooking. Eggplant, which comes from the Middle East, is part of many Greek dishes, such as **moussaka** (moo-suh-KAH). Fresh herbs such as dill, mint, and parsley are also used often in recipes.

Because most of Greece is near the sea, fresh fish is very popular.

13

olives

Greece is famous for its olives. Olive trees grow easily in the rough, rugged land of Greece. Their twisted, gray trunks can be seen all over the country. There are about 100 million olive trees there. Each tree lives for hundreds of years and grows many olives. Most trees produce olives each year. Some olive trees hadn't been cared for in the right way so now they might only produce olives every other year.

Green and black olives come from the very same olive tree. Black olives are just very ripe green olives.

Olive oil, of course, comes from olives. It is one of the most healthful cooking oils. People from the Mediterranean area often use olive oil in their cooking instead of butter.

The branch of the olive tree has been a symbol for peace for almost two thousand years. ▶

main dishes

Almost every city or town in Greece is close to the sea. Seafood such as crab, halibut, lobster, mussels, octopus, shrimp, and swordfish are part of many Greek meals.

Chicken too is an ingredient found in many recipes. It can be cooked in different kinds of stews, or a whole chicken might be broiled with just a bit of oregano and a squeeze of lemon juice.

Beef is not very popular in Greece. The land in Greece is very rocky, so there aren't enough grassy lands for cattle to feed on. Sheep are easier to raise than cattle in Greece. So when Greeks eat meat, they usually eat lamb. Lamb is often enjoyed as part of special meals during holidays.

◀ *There are more than 400 kinds of fish in the Mediterranean Sea. Many of them are used in Greek cooking.*

orektika

People snack on tasty treats on a **meze** (meh-ZAY) table a few hours before the midday meal or after a long day of work. Meze tables are covered with colorful, delicious dishes of ***orektika*** (or-tee-KAH), or appetizers. They are often set up in homes or small taverns. *Kalamata* olives, cheeses such as feta, *kefalotiri*, or *mizithra*, spiced meatballs, crunchy almonds, and crispy fried squid are just some of the things found on a meze table.

Greeks have enjoyed *orektika* for more than 2,000 years. It is an important part of their culture.

avgolemono
(egg-lemon soup)

you will need:

8 c. (2 l) chicken broth
1 c. (250 ml) uncooked
    rice
3 eggs
juice of 2 lemons
2 tsp. (10 ml) salt

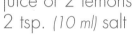

how to do it:

- In a large pot, bring broth to a boil over medium-high heat.
- Add rice, cover, and simmer on medium heat for 20 minutes.
- Remove from heat.
- Beat eggs well and add lemon juice to eggs while stirring.
- Slowly pour 1½ cups (375 ml) of hot chicken broth into egg-lemon mixture, stirring constantly.
- Add egg mixture to rest of broth-rice mixture. Continue to stir.
- Heat again without boiling.

- Serve with toasted pita bread. Serves 8

19

Always ask a grown-up to help you when using knives!
Always ask a grown-up to help you when using the stove or oven!

desserts

Sweets and desserts are a big part of Greek cuisine. But people don't usually eat dessert after an everyday meal. Sweets are usually eaten at **celebrations** (seh-luh-BRAY-shunz).

When a child is born, sweet cakes are given to all the people who come to see the family's new baby.

At weddings and other special parties, a famous Greek dessert called **baklava** (bah-kluh-VAH) is served. This rich dessert tastes as sweet as it smells. It is made with nuts and honey. You don't have to go to a Greek wedding to taste baklava, though. Many Greek restaurants and bakeries around the world serve this delicious dessert.

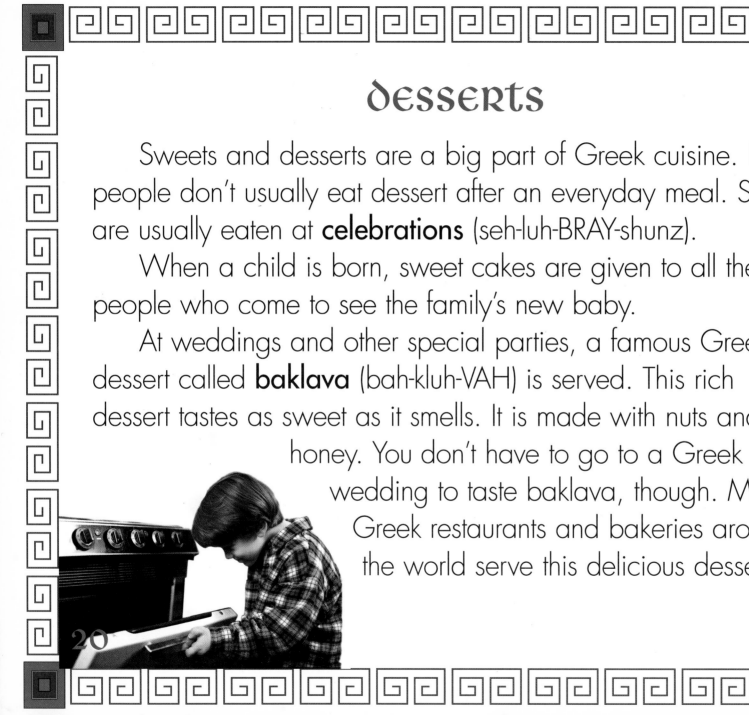

koulourakia
(greek cookies)

you will need:

¾ c. *(175 ml)* fine or sifted sugar

¾ c. *(175 ml)* vegetable oil

½ c. *(125 ml)* orange juice

½ tsp. *(2 ml)* baking soda

¾ tsp. *(3 ml)* baking powder

2 tsp. *(10 ml)* vanilla extract

2 c. *(500 ml)* flour

1 tsp. *(5 ml)* cinnamon

how to do it:

- Preheat oven to 400 degrees F. (200 degrees C.).
- In a medium mixing bowl, beat sugar and vegetable oil until smooth.
- Add orange juice, baking soda, baking powder, and vanilla extract. Stir well.
- In a separate bowl, mix the cinnamon and flour.
- Slowly add the flour mixture to the sugar mixture. Blend until dough is soft
- Spread a light layer of flour onto a smooth, clean surface.
- Place dough on the floured surface and knead until smooth.
- Break off walnut-sized pieces of dough and place evenly on a greased cookie sheet.

Bake for 12 to 15 minutes.   Makes 28 cookies.

Always ask a grown-up to help you when using knives!
Always ask a grown-up to help you when using the stove or oven!

greek food around the world

The **gyro** (YEE-roh), a Greek and Middle Eastern sandwich, has become very popular in many different countries. It is made from pita bread filled with lamb, beef, lettuce, tomato, and onion. It is served with a yogurt and cucumber sauce called ***tzatziki*** (taht-ZEE-kee). A recipe for *tzatziki* can be found in this book on page 11.

Greek cuisine can be found in restaurants all over the world. Because of this, many people have had the chance to try at least one popular Greek dish, such as *pastichio*, stuffed grape leaves, or *spanakopita*, a flaky spinach and cheese pie. But if any of your friends or family haven't tasted these dishes, now you can share the flavors of Greece with them.

Glossary

baklava (bah-kluh-VAH) A dessert made with nuts and honey.

celebration (seh-luh-BRAY-shun) A special time honoring something or someone special.

civilization (SIH-vih-lih-ZAY-shun) A group of people living in an organized and similar way.

cuisine (kwih-ZEEN) A style of cooking.

culture (KUL-cher) The beliefs, customs, art, and religion of a group of people.

explored (eks-PLORD) To have traveled over little-known land.

gyro (YEE-roh) A Greek and Middle Eastern sandwich made from a mix of beef and lamb that is served with vegetables in a pita.

meze (meh-ZAY) Small snacks, such as cheese or olives, that are served on a special table.

moussaka (moo-suh-KAH) A popular Greek dish made with eggplant and meat.

nutrient (NOO-tree-int) Anything that a living thing needs for energy or to grow.

orektika (or-tee-KAH) Appetizers, or snacks, that usually require cooking or more preparation than meze.

staple (STAY-pul) A very important and basic food item.

taverna (tah-VER-nuh) A cafe' in Greece.

tzatziki (taht-ZEE-kee) A cucumber and yogurt sauce.

index

B
baklava, 20
beef, 6, 17, 22

C
celebration, 20
cheese, 6, 9, 18, 22
   feta, 6, 18
chicken, 6, 17
civilization, 5
cucumbers, 13, 22
cuisine, 6, 13, 20, 22
culture, 8, 18

D
dessert, 20

E
eggplant, 13
explored, 8

F
families, 10, 22
fish, 6, 13, 17, 18

G
gyros, 22

H
holidays, 6, 17

L
lamb, 6, 17, 22
lemons, 13, 17, 19

M
markets, 13
meze, 18
moussaka, 13

N
nutrients, 6

O
olive oil, 5, 6, 14
olives, 5, 10, 14, 18
orektika, 18

P
pastichio, 22
pita bread, 22
potatoes, 6, 8

R
restaurants, 20, 22

S
spanakopita, 22
spinach, 13, 22
staple, 13

T
taverna, 10
tomatoes, 8, 13, 22
tzatziki, 22

Y
yogurt, 6, 10, 22